CRYPTOCURRENCY

TRADING

A CRYPTO INVESTING GUIDE

for Beginners

BITCOIN
ETHEREUM
LITECOIN

MEGALODONA STREAMINGS

TABLE OF CONTENTS

ECONOMY: GOLDEN RULES FOR INVESTING IN THE RIGHT WAY IN CRYPTOCURRENCIES

In this guide for newbies, I will try in the simplest way possible to give you the first notions in order to be able to invest in the cryptocurrency market. In the first part I will deal with the basics, in the second part you will find slightly more advanced tips and definitions, and in the final part we will take a dive into some winning strategies.

LET'S BEGIN!

Making money with crypto is no longer a novelty and the skepticism that many had surrounding crypto is now being met with an equal eagerness to participate. Forbes relayed the latest rankings of billionaires and revealed that more and more of them have expanded their fortune thanks to cryptocurrencies like Bitcoin - the original cryptocurrency.

To invest correctly you will need some rules and guidelines to take advantage of this opportunity, without incurring unnecessary risks. A few simple rules that allow you to accurately evaluate when and how to invest. This book also includes when and how to divest, to divert capital and profits to other assets and start making profits again.

To invest in cryptocurrencies, you must make conscious choices from the beginning, thus trying to put yourself in the most advantageous situation to reduce the risk of this trading.

Operate on regulated platforms

Before you start investing in cryptocurrencies, you need to decide which regulated platform you would like to use. The major centralized exchanges are similar to one another but may differ when it comes to costs, speed of action, safety and breadth of investment possibilities.

ALWAYS STAY UP TO DATE

The second rule of cryptocurrency trading is that information represents the maximum value: it is only thanks to correct and timely information that you can profit and avoid losses along with buying and selling at the most appropriate time. To do this, you need information on everything related to your cryptocurrencies. It is these channels of information that continually update us to keep an eye on the pulse of the situation.

PROTECT YOURSELF ON THE DOWNSIDE THANKS TO CFDS

Apart from investing directly in cryptocurrencies, you can invest in CFDs on cryptocurrencies. In this way it is possible to protect yourself in the event that the cryptocurrency in which you have decided to invest falls by recording a loss: they are called short positions and they allow you to earn when the purchase price of the cryptocurrency goes down, and lose when it goes up.

MAKE GOOD USE OF LEVERAGE

Remember that cryptocurrencies are quite volatile, this means that they can record considerable variations in a short time: if you make use of significant financial leverage, you can quickly gain large amounts but also lose equally large ones and with the same ease.

DIVERSIFY ACROSS DIFFERENT CRYPTOCURRENCIES

Investing by selecting a basket of cryptocurrencies is one of the most conservative strategies. Investing in a single asset is almost never advisable, it is always better to rely on no less than three or four different and unrelated cryptocurrencies.

STUDYING THE CRYPTOCURRENCIES TO INVEST IN

Knowing what your capital is going into is essential. Correct and always updated information is the first countermeasure against losses, and the most important tool to guarantee the desired profits. Ignoring this rule could lead to substantial losses. For example, it could be the case that you buy a very promising and reliable cryptocurrency without knowing that a Blockchain Fork operation is already underway concerning it, an operation which, as we will see shortly, can involve exceptional volatility.

KEEP AN EYE ON THE BLOCKCHAIN FORKS

You may remember that in the beginning there was only one cryptocurrency, Bitcoin, whose inventor also created the software behind the blockchain. Not long after, a second came, then a third and so on. One of the cryptocurrencies that followed the birth of Bitcoin is Litecoin: a very well-known and appreciated cryptocurrency today.

Not everyone knows that Litecoin began as a bifurcation of Bitcoin: its creators promoted a new token and convinced users to invest in the new Bitcoin clone virtual currency. Without getting into technicalities, this is always possible and when it happens you can witness a more or less momentary phenomenon of high volatility of the cryptocurrency concerned.

> As you will see, the rules are basically simple: following them consistently is essential to obtain rewarding results.

Cryptocurrency trading is not governed by universal laws that allow investors to always make money and never lose.

Losing money must be taken into account as a possibility or rather as a risk. However, there are rules that you can follow to protect yourself, because they prove to be really effective and take into account losses, capital management and last but not least, the emotional attitude in dealing with cryptocurrency trading.

Therefore, there are some golden rules that can help you during trading operations and that can teach you to do it well, without incurring unnecessary losses.

INVEST ONLY AS MUCH AS YOU CAN AFFORD TO LOSE

This means that you should not take a risk that you cannot afford, because it is possible to lose everything when you are investing in cryptocurrencies. Throwing yourself headlong into this type of market hoping to make money from the market itself can be a real disaster: consider that trading is inherently risky. When you establish an amount to invest in trading, you have to take the perspective that that amount is lost: legal regulations, software bugs or hacks could come into play so as to make you lose all your investment.

ESTABLISH THE "STOP LOSS"

Every new investor that is entering the market should be made well aware of a "Stop Loss". This allows you to minimize the potential loss of money in a specific plausible range.

Whenever you decide to take a position, you must be sure that you establish a Stop Loss that takes into account previous trends.

NEVER ACT ON IMPULSE

The moment you are aware that your trade is close to collapse, never make the blunder of impulsive trading, i.e., selling outright. Be aware that this is a temporary trend, so if you get emotional, price charts can be addictive and lead you astray; analyze the history of the currency you are interested in.

Reason that, by following your strategy and not making impulsive choices, you could lead avoid incorrect trades. Letting emotions replace rationality means ruining trading which, on the other hand, with calm and patience, can be synonymous with earnings.

Emotions play a key role: if you are experienced but emotional, you risk compromising the whole operation and throwing away your money.

AVOID OVERTRADING

Overtrading is a quite common mistake that traders make, in fact many cryptocurrencies' investors without experience make profits very quickly, then decide to invest the full amount right away hoping to gain additional profits. Alternatively, after losing they decide to invest larger amounts to recover the full amount and try to get their money back.

These are cases which are destined to end in bankruptcy, or to end with the loss of money.

KEEP UP TO DATE WITH BITCOIN PRICE FLUCTUATIONS

Cryptocurrencies must take into account the movement made by Bitcoin prices; if this rises, those of the others fall and this happens because investors decide they want to exchange Bitcoin with them.

The price of the Altcoin, on the other hand, also falls when that of Bitcoin does because the traders simultaneously exchange fiat cryptocurrencies. Basically, the exchange of cryptocurrencies must always take into account the price of Bitcoin.

You have to diversify

In the cryptocurrency market it is necessary to diversify, i.e., not invest exclusively in one type of currency, but manage the investment based on types. Even in this case, however, it is important not to throw yourself into it emotionally but to rationally evaluate the coins and not necessarily opt for low-cost ones hoping to earn important figures.

Practice using the demos

If you are a completely inexperienced investor, you must first practice using a demo account, to understand how to use cryptocurrencies and, only when you feel you are familiar with the trading markets, you can operate with a real account.

THE GOLDEN RULES

NEVER INVEST MORE THAN YOU ARE WILLING TO LOSE.

Really, don't do it! It must be your law to not invest more than you can afford to lose, to avoid catastrophic situations. Cryptocurrencies are still young, unregulated in some countries, and the market is extremely volatile. Prices rise and fall dramatically even within hours, if not minutes. Furthermore, there have been many cases of exchanges that suddenly close, ponzi schemes, scams and fake coins. When you invest money in the cryptocurrency market, consider it as money you've already lost from the start, this will help you to hold back the excitement of the moment.

When Ripple / XRP (but it happened with almost every coin), plummeted from nearly $4 to $1 in the early days of 2018, this post appeared on reddit to help those who had bought large quantities of XRP at a high price (for example, $3), convinced that the coin would continue to surge, only to find it on the floor. It sounds like a satirical message but instead it is serious: on that occasion there were a large number of calls to the hotline by people who wanted to commit suicide for having lost everything they had. And we have read about people who, to take advantage of the surge, took out loans or sold their cars and houses to invest everything and take advantage of the opportunity. Invest with extreme caution, especially if you are a beginner!

THE BEST TIME TO INVEST IN CRYPTOCURRENCIES IS YESTERDAY, AND TODAY.

Although there are those who manage to earn by carrying out small operations within a day (day trading), in the world of cryptocurrencies the bulk of the gains is made with long-term investments, from 2 to 5 years and beyond. The question that is asked most often when it comes to cryptocoins is: "But is it a good time to invest? Maybe I'll wait a little longer". The truth is that when a project behind a coin is valid, you can be sure that by the time you've had it five years, its value will have increased by 10, 100, if not 1000 times.

From $2 in 2014 to $70 in September 2017. And from that September, to almost $400 at the end of November. The madman who bought the LTC at $70 at the peak of September 2017 and then saw it reach $40 a few days later, how would he have reacted, in your opinion? A beginner would have sold everything to limit losses, while the expert, believing in the project, would have waited, knowing that sooner or later the market would reward him. And in fact.... look what happened next!

Buy The Rumor, Sell the News

This phrase literally means you should buy to rumors, sell to facts. This sentence hides the basis of any market strategy: anticipating the times and always keeping yourself informed. Suppose there is a big rumor, according to which, the big shot, Bitcoin, becomes the national currency of America. Obviously, an opulent investor waits for the news to become official before buying more Bitcoin, since such a thing, if true, would result in a large increase in the value of Bitcoin.

The real investor, however, begins to buy already in the previous phase: in this way, when the news is made official, the price of Bitcoin will have already risen, and completely counter-trend, he can sell his coins at a higher price than he purchased them at. What if the rumor is false? It doesn't really matter. The rule is so well established that even if the news were false, investors who buy at the end of the rumor raise the value of the asset themselves, generating a positive increment. So, denied or not, there is always a small fraction of a gain or at least very small losses. This introduces us to a very important concept that deserves a separate paragraph!

CRYPTOCURRENCIES AND THE EMOTIONAL MARKET

Finding out about the market trend is always a great idea, being aware of what banks, governments, the development teams behind the different cryptocurrencies are doing. However, the market trend almost never follows the trail of good or bad news, but rather a "sentiment" dictated by the emotional component of investors. If investors are afraid, they sell, if they are optimistic, they buy.

This is especially true in the coin market: if a coin is losing value, even amidst positive news, it will continue to lose value, until it reaches a point so low that it tempts investors to buy it at that reduced price. And at that point, a small hint of "green" after a red market is enough to unleash a chain reaction.

I wanted to highlight the word news because, as mentioned before, rumors, precisely because they are more irrational, have more influence on market sentiment. This is the case in what happened at the beginning of 2018: the sharp fall of ALL cryptocurrencies, with losses of up to 50-60%, due to a series of factors, above all the rumor that the Asian markets would ban cryptocoins, triggering panic selling.

So, do not be scared if the value of your favorite coin, despite any new partnerships, new adoptions, new updates, does not go up by a cent; on the contrary, its value is more likely to drop on this news, to allow large investors to buy more. But we will talk about market manipulations in the third part of the guide.

Now you are ready to get serious and go to the
second part of the guide!

SOME TERMS USED IN THIS BOOK:

Exchange: these are "exchange" sites, where users, once registered and verified, can exchange real currency (dollar, euro) into cryptocurrency.

Ponzi scheme: a scam in which the top management, consisting of just a few people, through bogus promises are able to earn money at the expense of many investors.

Day Trading: the practice of buying and selling an asset or a coin within the same day, leveraging small daily fluctuations.

Panic selling: a market behavior that occurs when, during a losing phase, investors sell massively for fear of increasing their losses even more, exacerbating an already negative market.

INTRODUCTION TO BITCOIN AND CRYPTOCURRENCIES

Have you heard your friends talk about Bitcoin?

Are you wondering what cryptocurrencies are and why everyone is talking about them lately?

Would you like to invest in the market and earn quickly?

YOU ARE IN THE RIGHT PLACE!

I state that earning in a short time with the crypto market, while possible, is obviously difficult.

Before getting into the market, it is good that you at least know the basics.

First of all, Bitcoin or cryptocurrencies in general are just the tip of the iceberg.

The real revolution in all of this, and which very few people know about, is the BLOCKCHAIN technology, a technology so revolutionary that it has been equated with the "discovery" of the internet. I will try to explain briefly and clearly, the basic concepts of the world of cryptocurrencies, in order to act with more awareness on the market. Let's go in order!

Blockchain Technology

Here the blockchain revolution begins. The blockchain is a decentralized data distribution network. In very simple terms, all the data in a database, instead of being kept in one "place", is scattered and fragmented in different places, linked together.

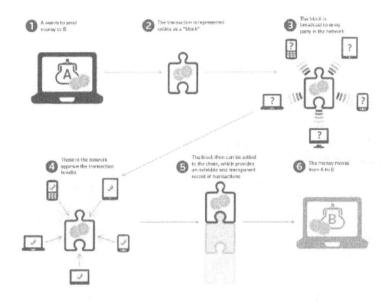

I'll give you a practical example. Let's consider, just to stay in the financial field, a bank. Each bank has its own database, or a set of data relating to its customers (personal data, account, deposits, etc.). This database is physically located on a server, which is a machine, similar to a computer, which is usually located in a safe place. Of course, anyone with access to the server can modify its data or in this case, steal customer account details and clean them out completely. The blockchain revolution consists, above all, in the security factor. If the same bank used the blockchain to store its data, the information would be stored, in a fragmented way, among thousands if not millions or billions of "nodes", all protected by cryptography. This means that the hacker who wants to steal some simple information, such as the surname of a customer, must be able to force access to ALL the nodes of the network to obtain, among other things, a single piece of information: a physically impossible job.

Decentralization allows all nodes to have equal power, unlike a centralized system where, as in our example, all data is stored in a single element. Each time data is recorded on the blockchain, the confirmation of the network nodes is required in order to verify that the recording of the data, or the "transaction", is secure. Several transactions are grouped into a block, which is connected to the previous block: hence the name blockchain. This implies that data cannot be deleted from a block, only added to the chain. Among other things, the whole blockchain, and therefore the set of transactions, is public: anyone can see where the data is recorded and when, but obviously the content is protected and not accessible.

The example of the bank is just one of the many applications of the blockchain, a technology that can be used in land registry, financial operations, but also in healthcare, ecommerce, music, video games and social media. Anything can be put on blockchain with a huge advantage in security, transparency, but above all in costs.

Cryptocurrencies

So, what is the relationship between Bitcoin and other cryptocurrencies if information is entered on the blockchain? Well, if the blockchain is the car, the coins are the gasoline. In fact, any data recorded on the blockchain is recorded as a "transaction". The registration of the transaction in a block is done by the Miners, companies or individuals who are in possession of powerful computers, which solve the algorithms necessary to record the transactions, encrypt them and add them to the chain. Obviously, nothing is done for free: miners are rewarded for the registration of transactions and for the creation of the blocks of the blockchain, with a small charge, called "fee". This fee is paid with virtual currency, which will be the currency of the blockchain in question.

For example, let's consider the Bitcoin blockchain. When person A sends person B Bitcoin, a transaction is queued in the blockchain network. The miners record the transaction on the block, and a tiny part of the Bitcoin sent is retained by the miner as compensation for the operation performed. Once the network has confirmed the security and veracity of the transaction, person B will have the Bitcoin in his or her account.

The value of Bitcoin, which has risen in a few years from cents to thousands of dollars, is dictated solely by the supply / demand of the market: the more people buy Bitcoin, because they believe in blockchain technology, the more the price goes up. And this concept is valid for all other cryptocurrencies.

The Cryptocurrency Markets

While Bitcoin began as a currency, there are many other coins that have different functions, based on the project and the platform behind it. Some coins can be used to buy electricity, to view certain content on the internet, to listen to certain music, the applications are really many and the technology is only in its infancy.

A crypto investor buys at the beginning of a "valid blockchain project" a certain sum of coins at very low cost (even in the order of one millionth of a cent). If the project is valid and grows over time, more people will need that coin to use the platform or service linked to the project, and therefore the availability of coins will decrease. This will create a big demand, and the price of the coin will go up. The investor can then sell his coins and make a fair profit, or use them himself for related services.

Obviously, there is still a lot to say, but these very few concepts expressed in a basic way should be enough for now.

You are now ready for the basics of the cryptocurrency market!

HOW TO BUY CRYPTOCURRENCIES

THE EXCHANGE: LOVE AND HATE, BUT ABOVE ALL HATE

The exchanges are companies that have a large number of crypto coins and that act as intermediaries for the exchange of crypto coins. Exchanges can be between FIAT money (i.e., real currency, dollar, or euro for example) and cryptocurrency, or between cryptocurrency and cryptocurrency. For each operation, be it an exchange, a deposit or a withdrawal, a small percentage of the currency is withheld by the site as a tax or fee. Even if the fee seems tiny (generally they are on the order of 0.1-0.2%), if you consider the traffic of billions of dollars on the exchange sites, you will understand that the earnings from the fees are mind-boggling. To buy cryptocurrency, what you need to do is open an account on a reputable exchange site, put money into it and then make the exchange. Each exchange has its own wallet, in which it will keep your coins, ready to be used. To buy cryptocurrency you just deposit FIAT currency in the account of the Exchange and then exchange with cryptocurrency. Easy, isn't it?

BEFORE YOU JUMP INTO IT, KEEP IN MIND THAT:

All exchanges, especially the serious ones, will ask you for different verification procedures: copies of multiple identity documents, photos, authentications on mobile phones, etc.

Cryptocurrencies left on exchanges and therefore in the wallet (or wallets) of the site are potentially at risk. In case of failure of the Exchange (as has happened with Bitconnect), all money paid will be lost with no hope of recovery.

The transaction fees are arbitrarily chosen by the exchange (those over and above the transition costs due to the miners). This means that for each coin, you should evaluate on which exchange there are lower fees, provided that the site is obviously reliable.

Exchange networks can go offline with little or no notice: therefore, the exchange or withdrawal operations could be temporarily suspended. Typically, this happens either due to an update of the software of a coin or due to network congestion.

There are few exchanges that allow the FIAT / crypto exchange, so you may have to sign up for more exchanges and do more exchanges to get a certain result.

DON'T INVEST MORE THAN YOU ARE WILLING TO LOSE!

This provocative title is given by the fact that in an already poorly regulated market, full of scams, exchanges offer very few guarantees, so you must be extremely cautious. To increase security, especially for those who have invested a fair amount of money, you can consider the idea of buying a hardware wallet such as the Ledger Nano S, a kind of electronic wallet similar to a USB pen in which to deposit your coins, so that you always have them with you rather than deposited on a site that you can only control so much.

The exchanges that I personally use are three, Coinbase, Binance, and Bittrex, but there are many others, relatively reliable. To start with, Coinbase is definitely the best ...

I HAVE MY FIRST COIN, NOW WHAT? **HODL!**

The term derives from a typo of Hold which soon went viral. Once you have bought the desired amount of cryptocurrency, you will obviously have to wait for its value to rise. To monitor the price, I recommend two sites, one is CoinMarketCap or CMC while the other is CoinGecko.

Pay close attention to the data that are shown on these sites: the prices are relative to an average of all the prices on the different exchanges. In fact, it may happen that this difference is sometimes really huge. This is the case especially of the Korean / Asian exchanges whose prices are generally higher and therefore positively influence the average value. For this reason, both CMC and CoinGecko allow you to exclude Asian values from the calculation of the average. Suppose, for example, that you have bought Bitcoin at $50,000 on Binance. The next day the price on CoinGecko is $55,000. Imagine you enthusiastically go back to Binance to sell, only to find that on Binance it is actually $48,000 and that the price increase was due to Korean exchanges where Bitcoin stands at $60,000!

So be very careful before selling.

Both CoinMarketCap and CoinGecko are information-rich sites.

For example, keep in mind that when you sell a coin, you sell it as part of the "mini market" of the Exchange. The sale price on Binance or Kucoin will be different, even if only slightly! The ranking of the coins is given by the Market Cap, a value that indicates the total "traffic" that revolves around that currency. I will talk more about this in the advanced part of the guide.

KNOWLEDGE IS POWER

The last tool you need to be a true novice crypto investor is knowing where to find information. I will not lie to you, unfortunately you need to have a minimum knowledge of English and the web to be able to make the most of the opportunity. On the other hand, we are talking about new computer technology. Personally, the sources I use are mainly Twitter, Reddit, and CoinGecko/CMC.

It seems absurd, but it is no coincidence that Twitter is the first source: being able to follow the developers behind each coin, influencers and big investors on the social network, you will often know the latest news before the industry newspapers do, and can draw your own conclusions.

Reddit is a very popular social forum, divided into several sections, one or more, for each coin. The information on Reddit must be filtered: users of a Bitcoin sub-Reddit will obviously be blindly in favor of Bitcoin and against the adoption of other currencies, and so on. A bad place to ask for advice, however Reddit is a great news aggregator: if there is a rumor or news about a coin, it will surely be reported on its sub-Reddit, making the task of finding information extremely easy.

You now have all the basic tools to start investing in the world of cryptocurrencies. The "how much" to invest obviously depends on your economic situation and how much you are willing to lose without catastrophic results.

If I really have to put my finger on a figure, in my humble opinion, a minimum initial investment could be $500, perhaps aiming at some valid coin that still costs a few cents, such as the TRX I wanted to buy this morning. The beauty of this world, however, is that it is all to be discovered, start reading and informing yourself and soon you will be the one to give me some advice!

USEFUL TERMS:

FIAT = real currency, such as dollars or euros

HODL = hold the coins instead of selling them, to wait for a better market moment

Bullish / Bull market = sudden positive market trend

Bearish / Bear market = negative market trend

FOMO = Fear of missing out. "Fear of missing the train". It is used to mean the purchase of a coin during a rising market because it is assumed that the market will continue the positive trend

FUD = "Fear, uncertainty, doubt". It indicates a moment of doubt in the market, in which, for fear of a collapse in values, one begins to sell, causing the collapse of the market itself (the so-called panic selling by FUD).

WALLET, ORDERBOOK AND ORDER TYPES

*We have reached the part of the guide in which
I will try to give you, in my opinion, the tools to
deal with a "critical market" and optimize
earnings.*

YOUR WALLET

If you have reached this part of the guide, I believe you have already started investing your first nest egg in cryptocurrencies. Depending on the amount of dollars invested, I advise you to start thinking about securing your coins, especially if you do not intend to exchange them soon. As mentioned above, keeping your coins on exchanges, no matter how reliable they are, is never 100% safe. There are several solutions to secure your coins, I personally feel I can recommend two.

The first, cheaper one, is to download a desktop wallet. It is a program that works as a wallet, which can be installed on your PC, from which you can safely send (or receive) your coins.

With a desktop wallet you will physically have the keys to your coins, so you will be the only ones to be able to control them, unlike what happens on exchanges. There are several desktop wallets out there, I personally used Electrum Wallet and I was fine with it until I moved on to the next step. Unfortunately, Electrum does not support all coins, and security, despite the password and recovery seed, still depends on the state of your PC (viruses, keyloggers, trojans, etc).

IN SUMMARY:

No cost

Easy to use

Safer than exchanges. Security depends on your PC. It does not support all coins

The second and safest option is to buy a hardware wallet. I did not buy a hardware wallet until the amount of my investment was sufficient to require it, also because it is a rather expensive device. A hardware wallet is an extremely secure wallet, because in addition to having different protection systems it is a cold wallet, or a key storage system that does not have access to the internet, so it is almost immune to viruses, hackers, scams and so on. I say almost, because to make the transactions you will have to temporarily connect it to the network, but the risks are still minimal. The two most famous hardware wallets are the Ledger Nano S and the Trezor Wallet. I recommend, in case you decide to buy one, to opt for the Ledger Nano S: it is cheaper but the quality is the same compared to the Trezor.

IN SUMMARY:

Extremely safe

Cost from 70 to 200 dollars

Relatively simple to use

It supports the most popular coins

Diversify!

In the world of cryptocurrencies, risks are always around the corner, and can affect even the most famous coins. For this reason, it is highly recommended to diversify your wallet by buying several different coins rather than going all in on just one. There are two main advantages to this type of scheme: the first is that in case your favorite coin goes wrong, the performance of the others can cushion the blow, allowing you to stay calm. The second advantage is that you can operate on different coins, thus taking advantage of a greater number of positive or negative changes in the market. You decide to what extent to diversify: in my wallet, for example, there are currently 5 different coins, which represent a percentage of my total investment of 40%, 30%, 10%, 10%, 10%. As you can see, I have two favorite coins, and three others that are long-term investments in the rather young ones. And then, don't forget an important thing: the beauty of this world is also to find out about the different projects and find the most promising ones!

OPTIMIZE PURCHASES AND SALES

In part 2 of the guide, we saw how, when buying a cryptocurrency, exchanges provide 3 types of orders: market, limit, stop or limit-stop. These types of orders are widely used in day trading or in any case by those who have extensive experience in the market and are able to predict price fluctuations. And then there are the whales ... but we'll talk about them later.

MARKET TYPE ORDER

Simple enough to understand: at the moment I submit the order, I buy the cryptocurrency with the current market price.

The drawback is that, from the moment I enter the amount I want to spend to the moment I send the order, the result obtained may be different because the market has fluctuated. As a result, I will end up with a lower (or higher) number of coins than expected at the start.

LIMIT TYPE ORDER

As the name suggests, the order is based on a set limit. It is used to buy or sell at a certain price threshold: it will be clearer with an example. Let's say we have 10 Bitcoin and the current market price is $60,000 per BTC.

LIMIT SELL

The limit sell is typically used in a growing market and serves to optimize revenue. Example: I want to sell my BTC assets, however at a price that I decide. With the Limit Sell, I set the limit price, which is the price to exceed in order for my order to be placed on the market. For example, by setting the limit price to $75,000, the system takes my 10 Bitcoin and places it in the order book - beware, even if you see the BTC disappear from your account, the sale has not yet been made and you can always go back! As soon as the market value of Bitcoin exceeds $75,000, my Bitcoin become available for other investors to buy. It is called limit because it is a threshold value: if, for example, with my 10 Bitcoin, I had to saturate the demand for Bitcoin already after having sold 7, the remaining 3 would be sold at a higher price, perhaps $77,000, earning even more!

LIMIT BUY

The limit buy is typically used in a falling market and is used to optimize purchases. Example: I have $600,000 and I want to buy 10 Bitcoin with that amount. Currently, the market price is $60,000, if I made a market order, I could only buy 10. But the market is sinking, I can't afford to check every second if it has reached the right price, so I send a limit buy order by setting the price to $55,000. The system then takes my $600,000 and places an order of 10 BTC in the order book. When the market price of BTC drops below $55,000, the system will start buying BTC to fill my order. In this case, if the supply of BTC exceeds the demand, it is likely that I will be able, with my order, to buy Bitcoin even at $53,000 or less!

STOP OR LIMIT-STOP TYPE ORDER

The STOP order is the quintessential save order. It is often associated with the limit, in order to make the procedure more precise. When you think about the stop order you have to think about this sentence: "STOP the loss of profit!" It is in fact a common order in a market that is negativizing and is used to "save" earnings. Example: after buying 1 Bitcoin at $60,000, the price skyrocketed to $100,000. However, yesterday it fell back to $90,000, today to $80,000. I have already lost $20,000 in potential earnings. Will it come down again? If it goes below $70,000, I want to sell it, but I don't want to sell it for less than $65,000, so that I can make a profit on my purchase of at least $5,000. It sounds like a middle school math problem, but it's the reasoning behind every STOP command. The STOP value indicates the price at which our coin will be placed on the market: in this case, we will enter the value of $70,000 as STOP. However, as I prefer not to sell below $65,000, I also enter the $65,000 limit. This means that, if the price drops below $70,000, my Bitcoin will be sold at a price ranging from $70,000 and $65,000.

ORDER OPTIONS

Sometimes on exchanges there are several options for placing orders. Sometimes they don't always have the same name, while still functioning the same. The most popular are "Good until Filled" and "Fill or Kill". With the "Good until Filled" option, the order remains in the book until it has been filled, i.e., until all the coins requested by me have been bought or sold. With the option "Fill or Kill" or "Fill or Cancel", if at the time of placing the order in the market, the order is not filled immediately, it is canceled. The usefulness of this last option lies in fulfilling the order immediately and at the price I set at the start, and serves to mitigate the fluctuations when buying with market-type orders.

MARKET TRENDS, CORRECTIONS AND PATTERNS

In the previous chapter we saw how important it is to diversify your wallet, how to optimize purchases and how the order book works. In this last part, we will deal with a much more advanced part, albeit in a basic way.

This will probably be the most important part, as we will go deeper into both the technical and the lesser-known part of price manipulation, trying to provide you with the basis for developing critical thinking and better addressing the volatility of cryptocurrencies.

MARKET ANALYSIS AND INVESTOR SENTIMENT

I state that I am absolutely not a market analyst, however as an enthusiast, following several users on Steemit too, I was able to get an idea of what signs may indicate a probable short- term rise in prices. I'll share with you that I have learned, it being understood that there are people much more qualified than me for this!

We repeat two main definitions: bullish market means a rising market; bearish market means a falling market.

That said, market analysis aims to be able to predict the trend of a market based on patterns that are repeated cyclically. But how do the patterns predict the future market trend if it is not possible to predict new technological developments, new collaborations or in general the positive and negative events that affect a coin?

As already mentioned elsewhere, the cryptocurrency market, in addition to being extremely volatile, is also emotional, i.e., it does not follow a logic dictated by positive or negative events, the more the sentiment of investors: fear or enthusiasm for a particular news article is much more important than the news itself!

New partnerships, new adoptions by exchanges, new updates to the platform, new features, openings to new markets; these are all events which, however, will not raise the price of a cryptocurrency. However, a rumor, such as that of China banning cryptocurrencies, is enough to make all markets collapse.

It is not the news that makes prices go up or down, but .... the buying or selling of coins by investors!

So, is the news useless? Absolutely not! Imagine if we didn't have news from the Bitcoin developers: investors would start thinking that the project is dead and then ... to sell, causing the price to plummet. Good news serves to stabilize prices, or at least to make the market around that coin active.

The technical analysis of a market is therefore totally independent of news, of any kind, even if it is not certain that these cannot influence prices. The analysis is simply based on studied patterns that have been repeated for decades, and which reflect the investor's behavior in certain situations.

I'll give you an extremely trivial example: imagine that you have a fair amount of a cryptocurrency, and that this cryptocurrency has a bang. After a noticeable price increase, what would you do? You obviously sell. There are those who perhaps sell everything, those who perhaps sell a part, those who sell and then at the first uptick buy back: in general, the feeling is that of selling.

Everyone will think the same thing, everyone will sell, and after a beautiful spike, the price of the coin will start to go down. Price reduction of 5%, 7%, 10%, 15%. Who had bought before the phase of growth of the price for FOMO, begins to be afraid because the profit margin is thinning, so he too sells, contenting himself with a low income.

The price then continues to fall, by 20%, by 30%, the FUD is triggered, investors begin to fear that the coin may go bankrupt, then it falls again, by 50% or 60% ... Why? Fortunately, there are experienced investors, who do not panic as they know the market trend, and because they know that it is precisely when there is a bearish market that purchases are made.

Those who sold at the peak, begin to buy back, also using their recent revenues and therefore buying a larger share of coins, new investors are attracted by the low price, we begin to glimpse the positive trend, 5%, 10%, 15%, then the FOMO is triggered, and everyone starts buying out of "fear of missing out". And when it reaches its peak, you already know what's going to happen, right?

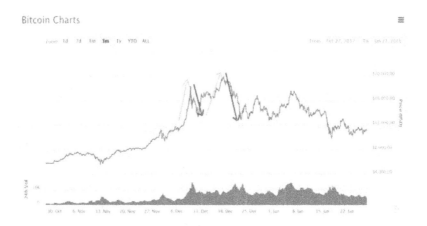

THE CORRECTIONS

Precisely because the cryptocurrency market is an emotional market, it often happens that a coin is extremely overvalued. This happens because with the right combination of factors, (for example whales, which I will talk about in the next part), an increase in the price can trigger the FOMO and consequently a chain reaction, that leads to a coin that is perhaps worth 10 cents selling at a price of 10 dollars. In general, such a disproportionate increase in price is determined by the entry into that market of investors who do not believe in the project or who do not want to invest in the long term: consequently, they buy with the sole purpose of selling as soon as possible. This initially results in an overvaluation and then a series of bounces, called corrections. Corrections are an extremely positive element for good, as they stabilize the price even if they drop it to values that are closer to the real ones.

Look at the example of Cardano / ADA, one of the coins with the most potential currently. After the ATH (All Time High) of $3.09, ADA underwent a correction that brought it steadily to around $2.00. In fact, Cardano at the time of the ATH had numerous features still in development, so such a high price was not justifiable. However, compared to being under a dollar at the beginning of 2021, ADA is still clearly growing and indeed, is probably now waiting to explode, given the numerous advances that the development team has made.

The corrections are therefore generally negative market trends, mostly short, which stop the price rise. Generally, there is a drop of about 10% and it is not uncommon to have, after this drop, a sudden increase in the price (caused by investors who buy to resell in the short term) followed by a further decline, cyclically, until stabilization. The more a price has been overestimated, the harder the correction will be, so much so that sometimes a bear market dictated by the FUD is triggered.

Patterns For Beginners

Here I'll show you the main patterns that I have learned to recognize.

CUP & HANDLE

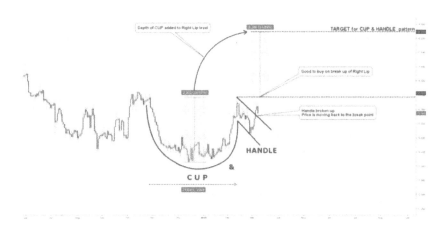

A bullish pattern occurs when, after a peak, there is a negativization followed by a long period of price stabilization. Then follows a further peak with a fall (the cup handle). This pattern typically indicates a subsequent rise to the handle equal to the depth of the cup.

HEAD & SHOULDERS

A bearish pattern occurs when, after a positive trend, 3 peak and correction cycles are formed. The first and third loops are the "shoulders", the middle loop taking the name of "head". The line that joins the two shoulder corrections is called the neckline. After this pattern, we expect a market negativization equal to the distance between the neckline and the peak of the head.

There is also a bullish pattern called Head & Shoulder Reversed, in this case there was a previous negative market, where the three negative shoulder and head cycles indicate a market close to bullish.

For now, I'll stop here, there is a lot to think about and I don't want to bore you with technicalities, which by the way is not the purpose of this article, since there are more qualified people than me. However, these patterns are very simple to recognize and can direct you towards a purchase or a sale, but above all they serve to stimulate your search.

WHALES, WALLS AND MARKET MANIPULATION

In this last part, which I consider the most important, I will talk about who are the actors behind the cryptocurrency market and what are the tricks that are used to control prices.

I will remind you of some terms: FOMO indicates the sentiment of investing during the price increase, FUD and panic selling are correlated and indicate the fear of investors that generates an increase in sales with a collapse in prices.

WHALES AND SMALL FISH

The term "Whale" indicates a large investor. To be clear, a large investor is a person or a company that has invested billions in a particular coin, and which, independently, is able to bring about a tangible positive or negative decline in prices. Let's consider Bitcoin for example: there are approximately 19 million in circulation, if I own 10 million, I can initiate good and bad times by selling and buying.

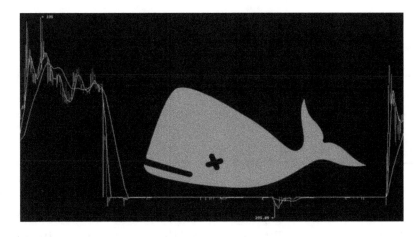

Next to the whales, there are us, the small fish, who, even if not consciously, adapt to the game of whales. In reality, whales are not always a bad thing, they are often responsible for a sudden rise in prices and therefore a profit for smaller investors.

Let's take Ripple / XRP for example. Ripple is a service designed to facilitate cross-border money movements, between states, in a very short time and at very low cost. If a bank wants to adopt XRP and the Ripple system for its transfers, it will buy a large sum of XRP, with investments of billions (as happened in November 2017) with a consequent price hike, triggered by FOMO, creating a further price growth.

WHO CONTROLS THE MARKET?

But who are the whales really? Individuals, banks, exchanges, founders of the coin. And these characters often coordinate their movements in order to exercise control. Look at the list, for example, of Litecoin / LTC holders:

Litecoin Rich List

block, address, transaction   Search

Share

Litecoin distribution

Balance	Addresses	% Addresses (Total)	Coins	$USD	% Coins (Total)
0 - 0.001	559549	24.43% (100%)	306.31 LTC	56,107 USD	0% (100%)
0.001 - 0.01	268416	11.72% (75.57%)	1,375 LTC	251,799 USD	0% (100%)
0.01 - 0.1	364060	15.89% (63.85%)	12,134 LTC	2,222,581 USD	0.02% (100%)
0.1 - 1	435642	19.02% (47.96%)	185,387 LTC	33,957,820 USD	0.34% (99.97%)
1 - 10	440806	19.24% (28.94%)	1,481,535 LTC	271,376,612 USD	2.7% (99.64%)
10 - 100	186524	8.14% (9.7%)	5,541,143 LTC	1,014,985,655 USD	10.08% (96.94%)
100 - 1,000	32127	1.4% (1.55%)	7,761,612 LTC	1,421,714,848 USD	14.12% (86.86%)
1,000 - 10,000	3022	0.13% (0.15%)	7,395,509 LTC	1,354,654,756 USD	13.45% (72.74%)
10,000 - 100,000	331	0.01% (0.02%)	8,225,613 LTC	1,506,707,035 USD	14.96% (59.29%)
100,000 - 1,000,000	70	0% (0%)	24,365,557 LTC	4,463,102,714 USD	44.33% (44.33%)

Almost 50% of the LTCs are owned by only 70 people, and we are talking about 4 and a half billion dollars. If you are curious, on the Bitcoininfocharts website you can check the very rich also for the other coins.

HOW ARE PRICES MANIPULATED?

Selling and buying large amounts of a coin, triggering successive FOMO or FUD, is just the tip of the iceberg. There are other, less visible and more subtle mechanisms that play an even more important role.

BULK PURCHASE AND FOMO

This movement requires the collaboration of small fish, who, unaware, follow the sentiment dictated by the whales. If I see a growth of 5% for 3 days in a row, the enthusiasm rises and everyone buys, there will be a massive increase, even of 1000% in a few days: obviously the whales who bought first, when they sell, will be the ones who will earn more.

BULK SALE AND FUD

At a stable price, on the other hand, a sudden sale that leads to a decrease of 5%, 10% 15% day after day, triggers the opposite mechanism, fear, with consequent sale by the small fish. But why should whales devalue a coin they own, selling it for no apparent reason? Obviously to buy it back, at a reduced price and therefore increasing their share of coins.

Buy wall and Sell wall

Whales control the market mainly with buy walls and sell walls. It involves placing very large orders in the order book that constrain the price in a certain range.

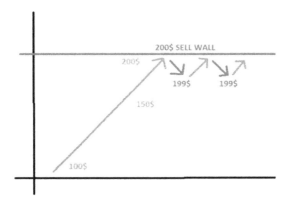

In the example, the sell wall is set at $200. This means that whoever wants to sell the coin must sell it for less than $200 to get over the wall. Whoever wants to sell at $201 must wait until all the coins placed at $250 are sold, which in most cases is impossible given the huge number of coins available to the whales. The result is that the price remains below $200 since every time the price goes to $200, a portion of the coin of the sell wall is sold, returning the price to $199.

A buy wall, on the other hand, has the opposite effect: it prevents the price from dropping too much. In the example, as soon as the falling price touches the $100 buy wall, coins are bought, causing the price to rise above $100.

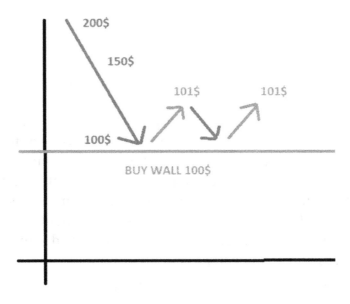

The union of buy wall and sell wall determines that the price of a coin is controlled and it cannot descend or rise outside certain thresholds. But why? In most cases the answer is given by the inherent use of the coin. I bring you a current example, that of Ripple / XRP.

This is how the orderbook of Ripple looks, whose price was stable for weeks, at around $1.30. The arrows indicate the different walls that allow this result:

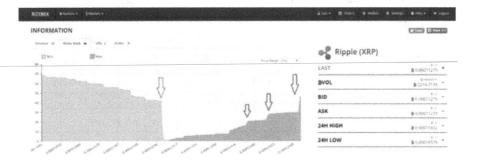

Although they are speculations, the reason for Ripple's price control seems to be given to allow banks to be able to buy large quantities once the tests on the Ripple platform are concluded. Too high a price means buying fewer coins from banks; too low a price means attracting other big investors who could reduce the stock of XRP for banks (XRPs are present in limited quantities in circulation). These are only theories, however, rest assured that if there is such evident manipulation on a coin, it means that the big shots have bet on it and is therefore a further confirmation of the validity of a project.

FAKE NEWS

It seems that investors are much more sensitive to bad news than to good news (since in the first case you might lose money). Influencers have a big effect in the cryptocurrency community and often news and rumors come from them, most of which are false. In the remaining cases, the influencers act as repeaters, through which fake news is transmitted to users, spreading panic and causing the collapse of prices. This is what happened in January with the possible ban on cryptocurrencies in Asian markets, or even earlier, what happened when we talked about the Bitcoin hard fork. However, as the golden rules of cryptocurrencies teach us, buy the rumor, sell the news, so it is precisely in these cases of manipulated collapse that the real investor buys.

I hope this book will be useful for your next purchases.

Now you should have all the basics to be able to face the market with more awareness and above all to deepen your knowledge.

WHAT ARE THE CRYPTOCURRENCIES TO BUY TODAY? THE COMPLETE GUIDE TO INVESTING IN 2021

A step-by-step guide to enter the world of cryptocurrencies as an investor. Find out how to really make money and which are the best websites to get you started.

Since the launch of Bitcoin in 2009, cryptocurrencies have literally revolutionized the way people invest. 2021 started under the best auspices for the digital currency market, and many investors are wondering how to invest in cryptocurrencies.

- ✓ Best Cryptocurrency of 2021: Dogecoin (+ 8,000%)
- ✓ Best Cryptocurrency Ever: Bitcoin (+20 million%)
- ✓ Best Cryptocurrency Exchange: 2021 Binance

While Bitcoin remains the most popular cryptocurrency, there are many more on the rise that investors should consider. But with such a large list of cryptocurrencies on the market, how do you go about choosing the best cryptocurrency to invest in?

WHAT DOES IT MEAN TO INVEST IN CRYPTOCURRENCIES IN 2021? If you are new to the world of cryptocurrencies, let me tell you what you absolutely need to know before investing in cryptocurrencies in 2021.

WHAT ARE CRYPTOCURRENCIES?

Before asking ourselves which cryptocurrency to buy today, let's take a step back to understand what cryptocurrencies are and how they work.

A cryptocurrency is a digital currency that uses blockchain technology to validate online transactions through decentralized systems. Thanks to blockchain technology, all cryptocurrency transactions are transparent, safe, traceable and irreversible.

Cryptocurrencies do not physically exist, but are "stored" in a digital wallet. A cryptocurrency wallet is software or an application that you can use to store, send and receive cryptocurrencies.

HOW CRYPTOCURRENCIES WORK

In fact, you can use cryptocurrency to transact within a network or exchange money between individuals, without the need to go through an intermediary. Cryptocurrencies are almost always designed to be independent and not governed by a central authority, such as a government or financial institution. This key feature has also made them extremely popular as a long-term investment for those who see a greater use of decentralized finance in the future.

WHEN WERE CRYPTOCURRENCIES STARTED?

In October 2008, a white paper was published by a mysterious author named Satoshi Nakamoto. This paper introduced a decentralized network used to power a new cryptocurrency called Bitcoin. Even before it was accepted as a new form of payment, Bitcoin had slowly begun to rise in price. Following the birth of Bitcoin, other cryptocurrencies were then launched.

HOW MANY CRYPTOCURRENCIES ARE THERE? HOW MUCH ARE THEY WORTH?

To date, around 15,000 cryptocurrencies exist, according to CoinMarketCap.com. Bitcoin is the most popular cryptocurrency, followed by Ethereum, Binance Coin and Dogecoin.

TOP 10 CRYPTOCURRENCIES BY MARKET VALUE

- ✓ Bitcoin 768.71B 40,849.63 (-3.67%)
- ✓ Ethereum 322.74B 2,745.37 (-5.04%)
- ✓ Cardano 69B 2.15 (-7.32%)
- ✓ Tether 68.34B 1.00 (+ 0.07%)
- ✓ Binance Coin 54.54B 324.39 (-7.83%)
- ✓ XRP 38.37B 0.894304 (-4.89%)
- ✓ Solana 37.16B 125.18 (-10.75%)
- ✓ USD Coin 29.24B 0.998987 (-0.01%)
- ✓ Dogecoin 25.99B 0.198115 (-4.78%)
- ✓ Polkadot 24.24B 27.00 (-11.06%)
- ✓ Prices in billions of USD

The market value of cryptocurrencies as of May 12, 2021 is approximately $2.5 trillion. The value of Bitcoin is approximately $1 trillion (about 40% of the market total).

BUY CRYPTOCURRENCIES

67% of eToro CFD users lose money when trading CFDs with this operator. Please consider if you are in a personal financial situation that allows you to lose money.

WHY INVEST IN CRYPTOCURRENCIES?

Cryptocurrencies are an increasingly tempting investment for a variety of reasons.

CURRENCIES OF THE FUTURE

In an increasingly connected and internet-based world, cryptocurrencies can become the currencies of digitization. This will inevitably lead to greater demand for cryptocurrencies. Many investors buy them in anticipation of their appreciation in value, and their independence from governments and central banks. Some cryptocurrencies are "rare" commodities, that is, they have a fixed supply quantity that cannot be altered by a central authority. Unlike fiat currencies, such as the dollar, euro, pound, etc., more cryptocurrencies cannot be "printed" by a central bank.

INFLATION PROTECTION

If inflation were to rise, cryptocurrencies would be a haven for preserving purchasing power. As this is an asset that cannot be manipulated, the price of cryptocurrencies could appreciate in times of inflation, as happens with gold.

BLOCKCHAIN TECHNOLOGY

Blockchain, the technology behind cryptocurrencies, is one of the reasons why many have decided to invest in cryptocurrencies. The blockchain is a decentralized transaction processing and recording system and can be more secure than traditional payment systems.

SPECULATION

Some speculators like cryptocurrencies because they are rising in value and can thus they continue to grasp the growth trend of these assets. Their extreme volatility is also a source of intraday speculation with short selling permitted by the best brokers on the market.

Obviously, Bitcoin's dominance is always evident, but its leadership is constantly decreasing, now close to 40%.

HOW TO INVEST IN CRYPTOCURRENCIES?

Do you want to invest in cryptocurrencies such as Bitcoin or Ethereum but don't know how to do it? Don't worry, it's a lot easier than you think.

There are two ways to buy cryptocurrencies:

- ✓ Via a cryptocurrency exchange (real cryptocurrency purchase)
- ✓ Via a broker's platform (CFD trading)

When you buy cryptocurrency at an exchange, you effectively own the cryptocurrency and can store it in a digital wallet.

Once you have bought a cryptocurrency, you will presumably wait for its price to rise before you can resell it, making a profit. Alternatively, you can use it as a form of payment, or to convert it into other cryptocurrencies.

Through the trading platform of an online broker, you can alternatively invest in CFDs on cryptocurrencies.

A CFD (Contract for Difference) is a derivative product that fluctuates based on the prices of an underlying asset, in this case a cryptocurrency. It is an operation between broker and trader, with which the former agrees to pay the difference in value of an underlying between two dates: the opening and closing dates of the contract.

Investing in CFDs on cryptocurrencies has a purely speculative purpose. You can decide to open a long position (speculating that the price will rise) or a short position (speculating that the price will decrease).

For example, when you open a long position on a Bitcoin CFD, you are speculating on the appreciation of the BTC / USD exchange. Conversely, if you go short on the Bitcoin CFD, you are speculating on the fall in the price of the BTC / USD pair.

THE COSTS OF INVESTING IN CRYPTOCURRENCIES

Even if cryptocurrencies are not controlled by any bank or institution, their networks have costs and the platforms that allow access to them do not work for free. We've summarized the costs and other features that can help you choose the right platform for you:

eToro - Capital.com - Binance - Libertex

- ✓ Minimum deposit: $50/ $20/ $1/ $10
- ✓ Platform level: Suitable for all / For experts / For experts/ Advanced users
- ✓ Commissions: 0%/ 0%/ 0.1%/ 0.6%
- ✓ Spread (BTC): 0.75%/ 0.5%/ Zero/ Zero
- ✓ Demo Account: $100,000/ $1,000/ None/ $50,000 Copy Trading Yes/ No/ No/ No

Today, the costs of buying cryptocurrencies, especially Bitcoin, are less than 1%. Much less than any traditional currency exchange might require. Just follow a few simple steps to start investing in cryptocurrencies. Here we have summarized the steps required with eToro.

1. REGISTER ON ETORO

Registering on eToro is free and is a rather quick procedure. Going to the official eToro website and clicking on the "Register Now" button will start a procedure that takes no more than 2 minutes.

Just enter: Username, email address and password. Then you accept the Terms and the privacy policy and click on "Create account". Alternatively, you can log in with your Facebook or Google account.

2. MAKE YOUR FIRST DEPOSIT

Confirm your identity by email and you will be able to make your first deposit. The minimum amount to start on eToro is $200. You can then make deposits as low as $50.

The payment methods provided by the platform are:

- ✓ Credit / debit card
- ✓ PayPal
- ✓ Skrill
- ✓ Trustly
- ✓ Rapid Transfer
- ✓ Wire transfer
- ✓ Neteller
  If you pay in dollars, or currencies other than the US dollar, the amount will be automatically converted by eToro according to the current exchange rate.

3. SEARCH FOR CRYPTOCURRENCIES ON THE PLATFORM

After making your first deposit, you can finally search for cryptocurrencies on eToro. You can type the name of the digital currency on the search bar, eg. BTC, or click on the left on "Markets", and then on "Crypto", to browse the list of cryptocurrencies available on the platform.

4. INVEST IN BITCOIN

After clicking on "Buy", a page will open with some information on Bitcoin.

There you will be able to view the feed of ideas shared by other investors, the statistics and the graph of the stock price. Now you will have to click on "Invest" at the top right.

Make sure you have selected the "Invest" box at the top, enter the amount you want to invest: with eToro you can invest in cryptocurrencies with a minimum of 50 dollars.

Finally, click on the "Open Position" button.

eToro is the world's leading social trading platform and offers a wide range of tools for investing in financial markets and cryptocurrencies.

It is a highly reliable broker as it is regulated and supervised by First Level Financial Institutions (CySEC). It also performs three functions in one: cryptocurrency broker, exchange and wallet. Everything you need to start investing.

eToro's investment platform is one of the most advanced and convenient for investing in cryptocurrencies, in fact over 20 million users worldwide have chosen eToro to invest.

eToro does not charge any deposit or trading commission apart from the spread, i.e. the difference between the sell and buy price. Spread costs on cryptocurrencies range from a minimum of 0.75% on BTC to a maximum of 4.5% on MIOTA.

Buying cryptocurrencies on eToro is very simple thanks to a wide range of payment options, including wire transfers, credit cards and Paypal.

eToro is the only online broker that offers both the ability to buy the underlying asset and to invest in cryptocurrency CFDs.

Furthermore, one of the main advantages of eToro is given by CopyTrading. Thanks to this feature it is possible to automatically copy the portfolios of the best-performing traders on the platform.

THERE ARE 29 CRYPTOCURRENCIES AVAILABLE ON ETORO:

Bitcoin (BTC)

Ethereum (ETH)

Ripple (XRP)

Dogecoin (DOGE)

Binance Coin (BNB)

Bitcoin Cash (BCH)

Ethereum Classic (ETC)

Litecoin (LTC)

Dash (DASH)

Stellar Lumens (XLM)

NEO (NEO)

EOS (EOS)

Cardano (ADA)

IOTA (MIOTA)

Zcash (ZEC)

TRON (TRX)

Tezos (XTZ)

Chainlink (LINK)

Uniswap (UNI)

Dogecoin (DOGE)

yearn.finance (YFI)

AAVE

Compound (COMP)

Decentraland (MANA)

Basic Attention Token (BAT)

Polygon (MATIC)

Enjin (ENJ)

Maker (MKR)

Shiba Inu (SHIB)

CAPITAL.COM

Capital.com is an online broker that was founded in London in 2016 and is regulated in several jurisdictions, including the UK, Cyprus and Belarus.

Capital.com's product offering is one of the largest on the market. The broker offers access to CFD trading on over 2,400 assets, including:

20 indices

68 cryptocurrencies

25 raw materials

2,155 shares

135 currency pairs.

One of the biggest benefits of trading with Capital.com is the educational section, with trading guides, educational material and access to the latest news.

Additionally, Capital.com offers a mobile app that leverages artificial intelligence (AI) in order to enhance the trading experience. It is one of the few brokers that uses this technology to help its traders.

BINANCE

Binance is the largest cryptocurrency exchange in the world by trading volume.

A cryptocurrency exchange like Binance allows you to deposit money in fiat currencies (euro, dollar, pound, etc.) and trade cryptocurrencies directly.

Binance is certainly suitable for more experienced investors who want advanced trading options to execute their cryptocurrency investment strategies. The "lite" version of Binance is still quite intuitive even for less experienced investors.

Binance is available both as a web-exchange and as an app, from which you can conveniently buy and sell cryptocurrencies with a simple click.

Overall, Binance offers over 500 cryptocurrencies, including its Binance Coin token, and the fees are quite low.

COINBASE

Coinbase is one of the most popular cryptocurrency exchanges in the world. Founded in 2012, it is a fully regulated and licensed exchange in the United States.

Coinbase is also ranked among the best cryptocurrency exchanges in the world for traffic, liquidity and trading volumes.

In April 2021, Coinbase became the first U.S. crypto trading company listed on the stock exchange. The initial public offering (IPO) valued the company at approximately $86 billion.

Coinbase is perhaps one of the simplest and most intuitive exchanges for investing in cryptocurrencies. It's easy to sign up and buy cryptocurrencies in minutes.

Coinbase offers around 60 cryptocurrencies to invest in and has plans to add more to the list.

BITPANDA

Bitpanda is one of the best exchanges for those looking for reliable platforms to buy cryptocurrencies.

Formerly known as Coinimal, it's a fintech company based in Vienna, specializing in the sale and purchase of Bitcoin and other cryptocurrencies.

Today it is one of the fastest emerging options in Europe to buy Bitcoin, Ethereum, Ripple and more. Currently there are only 16 cryptocurrencies present, but it allows you to exchange them directly with Fiat currency.

Bitpanda is a suitable exchange for both newbies and cryptocurrency investment experts.

Bitpanda commissions for buying and selling cryptocurrencies are 1.49% maximum. However, the costs are already built into the real- time price, so they are somewhat invisible to the user.

LIBERTEX

Libertex is a very competitive commission trading platform regulated and supervised by the Cyprus Securities and Exchange Commission (CySEC).

Libertex has over 20 years of experience and today boasts around 2.2 million users worldwide.

Libertex offers its users the opportunity to trade through the following assets:

- Over 50 currency pairs
- More than 100 shares
- Over 50 cryptocurrencies
- 18 stock market indices
- 17 Commodities
- 10 ETFs

The minimum deposit of $20 makes the Libertex platform very accessible even for those approaching the world of cryptocurrency investments for the first time.

The payment methods available on Libertex are PayPal, credit / debit card, wire transfer, Skrill, Neteller, paysafecard and Rapid Transfer.

The Libertex platform offers over 50 cryptocurrencies to invest in, including Bitcoin and a wide range of altcoins.

In terms of costs, Libertex is a fairly inexpensive broker. Libertex does not apply the spread between the sale and purchase price of the instrument, but rather a commission when opening the position.

In the case of Bitcoin, the commission applied by Libertex is 0.8%, but it can also go up to over 4% for less traded cryptocurrencies.

IS IT WORTH INVESTING IN CRYPTOCURRENCIES IN 2021? Investing in cryptocurrencies in 2021 requires a number of considerations to try to get the most out of your invested capital.

The main reasons to invest in cryptocurrencies in 2021 depend on:

- Supply and demand
- Risk appetite of investors
- Increased adoption of blockchain projects
- Being open to institutional investors

Investing in cryptocurrencies can clearly make a lot of money in the medium term. There are many investors who use cryptocurrencies as a tool to increase their wealth over the years.

The history of Bitcoin is an example of this: 100 dollars invested in Bitcoin in 2010, today it would be about 98 million dollars.

Cryptocurrencies are an excellent investment to capture the growth in demand for digital currencies, as more and more companies want to adopt the blockchain.

In the US, PayPal recently announced that it is accepting cryptocurrencies as a form of payment. Companies like Tesla and Square have made significant investments in Bitcoin, further legitimizing cryptocurrencies.

In the short term, many investors look to Bitcoin and cryptocurrencies as a safe haven asset to counter distrust of modern financial systems, especially in recent years, when central banks have continued to print paper money, flooding the system with liquidity to fight the various economic and financial crises. As a consequence, the value of fiat currencies (dollar, euro, yen or pound) did nothing but decrease against real assets (gold, cryptocurrencies, houses etc ...).

To cope with the increased demand for cryptocurrency investment from investors, traditional brokers are also opening their doors to the world of cryptocurrencies.

WHAT ARE THE RISKS OF INVESTING IN CRYPTOCURRENCIES?
Without a doubt, cryptocurrencies are a popular investment

among investors, but unfortunately, success isn't as easy as it sounds.

The value of Bitcoin and other cryptocurrencies tends to fluctuate a lot. You may see daily price movements of the order of 10% or higher.

Clearly this volatility could make you nervous and lead you to emotional mistakes. For example, you can sell when the cryptocurrency has dropped a lot, and then repent immediately after it rises again.

Other cryptocurrency risks depend on the regulation and functioning of exchanges. It is not uncommon, in fact, to read news of controls on exchanges by governmental authorities. Or, in some cases, sudden malfunctions of exchanges may occur that make it impossible to operate in cryptocurrencies. In the past, there have even been hacks that have stolen from users' wallets.

Other concerns about investing in cryptocurrencies hinge on their energy consumption and the risks of government emission policies. The Bitcoin network uses more electricity every year than all of Argentina, as a study carried out by the University of Cambridge indicates.

Finally, several central banks are looking into the idea of creating their own digital currencies. This would clearly create more competition for cryptocurrencies.

ADVANTAGES AND RISKS OF INVESTING IN CRYPTOCURRENCIES

- Transparency
- Secure and encrypted transactions
- Scarcity (fixed offer)

- Independence from central authorities
- Increased adoption of blockchain projects
- Volatility
- Regulation
- Malfunction of exchange
- Energy consumption

5 Secrets to Successfully Investing in Cryptocurrencies

There are assumptions that anyone looking to invest in cryptocurrencies should consider. We have summarized them in 5 key concepts.

1. UNDERSTAND THE CONCEPT OF CRYPTOCURRENCY

First, it is important for you to thoroughly understand the concept of cryptocurrency. Don't throw yourself into investing in something you don't understand. Therefore, the first thing you should do is study the world of cryptocurrencies, and the assets you intend to invest in.

Each crypto has a project (whitepaper) and its success always derives from the quality of the technological project behind it, except for Dogecoin.

2. ANALYZE THE CRYPTOCURRENCY MARKET

What is the most sought-after cryptocurrency at the moment? What is the value of that currency? Which cryptocurrency is increasing its market cap? Which cryptocurrency offers the best investment opportunity?

Ask yourself these questions and analyze the cryptocurrency market in detail to have a successful strategy. Follow the news faithfully and keep up to date on the latest events.

3. USE VOLATILITY TO YOUR ADVANTAGE

Price fluctuations can be very relevant for Bitcoin and other cryptocurrencies. However, volatility also offers significant opportunities for big gains. If a cryptocurrency has dropped a lot, but its potential hasn't changed, it could represent a buying opportunity at more attractive prices than before. Furthermore, many cryptocurrencies have a correlation with the trend of Bitcoin or Ethereum.

4. DIVERSIFY = INVEST IN MULTIPLE CRYPTOCURRENCIES

If you decide to invest in just one cryptocurrency, what happens if the currency suddenly collapses? This is not a wise strategy, to invest all your money in a single digital currency.

A well-balanced, diverse cryptocurrency wallet minimizes risks. What you could lose on one cryptocurrency, you can still earn with others.

5. START SMALL AND MAKE RECURRING INVESTMENTS

The first time, you don't necessarily have to start investing thousands of dollars. Start with a small position of a few hundred dollars, and then increase your investments little by little.

Observing the market regularly will give you greater awareness of the various assets. And as mentioned before, you can take advantage of periods of volatility to accumulate more investments at lower prices.

Cryptocurrencies To Invest In, In 2021

Let's see what are the digital assets to focus on this year. Both for those who aim at medium-term investments and for those who are considering a long-term investment.

Bitcoin (BTC)

Bitcoin is digital gold

The queen of the market is a decentralized cryptocurrency created in 2008 by a still unknown person who used the alias Satoshi Nakamoto.

It was launched shortly after, in January 2009, and has dominated the cryptocurrency market ever since.

Bitcoin is a peer-to-peer cryptocurrency, which means that all transactions occur directly between network participants, without intermediation. In Nakamoto's own words, Bitcoin was created to allow "sending payments online without going through a financial institution".

The big advantage of Bitcoin comes from the fact that it was the first cryptocurrency to appear on the market. Bitcoin has a limited maximum supply of 21,000,000 which makes it a store of value, like gold, rather than a currency.

Bitcoin is in fact now widely recognized by investors as a safe haven asset against inflation and macroeconomic instability.

More than a decade after its inception, Bitcoin continues to remain at the top of the cryptocurrency market. Bitcoin has a market capitalization of over $1 trillion, which means that Bitcoin accounts for around 45% of the cryptocurrency market.

Ethereum (ETH)

Ethereum is an open source decentralized blockchain system that has its own cryptocurrency, Ether.

The big advantage of Ethereum is that it is the ideal platform to execute smart contracts using blockchain technology. Smart contracts are programs that automatically perform the actions necessary to make agreements between two or more parties directly on the Internet, without intermediaries.

Unlike Bitcoin, Ethereum's total supply is not limited. This, on the one hand, certainly makes it more usable due to the growing demand, but on the other hand, it is also not at all "rare".

Ethereum is today the second most capitalized cryptocurrency with a total value of around 500 billion dollars.

Binance Coin (BNB)

BNB is the cryptocurrency launched by the homonymous exchange Binance.

Binance is one of the largest cryptocurrency exchanges globally and BNB experienced a significant price hike in early 2021, which put it on the radar of countless investors.

Ripple (XRP)

XRP was created by Ripple Labs as a quick, less expensive and more scalable alternative to existing cross-border payment systems such as SWIFT.

The main advantages of XRP are speed and safety. In fact, validating transactions within the XRP ledger is extremely fast as it takes about 5 seconds. This aspect makes it one of the most used cryptocurrencies for transactions between individuals.

Ripple coin is powered by mathematical algorithms and obeys fixed rules that cannot be changed. This is what makes XRP safe and reliable. No intermediary or organization controls XRP, and therefore it cannot be forged or duplicated.

Dogecoin (DOGE)

Dogecoin (DOGE) is a cryptocurrency that is based on the popular Internet meme "Doge" and features a Shiba Inu on its logo. The total supply of DOGE is not limited, which means that there is no limit to the number of Dogecoins that can be created. Dogecoin was primarily used as a reward system on

Reddit and Twitter to reward the creation or sharing of quality content.

The great popularity of Dogecoin is probably due to Tesla CEO, Elon Musk, who never hid his appreciation of DOGE in his tweets.

Dogecoin experienced exponential growth in the first four months of 2021, returning more than 8,000%. Many members of the cryptocurrency community use the phrase "To the Moon!" to describe the general sentiment of the growing value of Dogecoin.

Uniswap (UNI)

A decentralized trading protocol, known for its role in facilitating automated token trading in decentralized platforms (Dex). Uniswap was launched in November 2018, but in 2021 it gained considerable popularity thanks to the DeFi phenomenon. The creator of the Uniswap platform is Hayden Adams, one of the developers of Ethereum, with the aim of solving the problems that decentralized platforms have experienced with liquidity.

The total supply of the UNI token is 1 billion units. These will be available over the course of four years from the introduction of Uniswap. Subsequently, Uniswap introduced a "perpetual inflation rate" of 2% to maintain participation in the network.

Cardano (ADA)

Cardano is a blockchain platform launched with the aim of enabling innovators and visionaries to make positive global changes. It was founded in 2017 and ADA is the cryptocurrency based on the Cardano platform. Cardano is one of the largest blockchains to successfully use a consent mechanism proof-of-stake, which requires much less energy than the algorithm proof-of-work used by Bitcoin and Ethereum. In terms of offering, the maximum amount available of ADA is 45 billion. Overall, around 16% of ADA's total offering went to the project's founders, while the remaining 84% was split among investors, including 30% that has yet to be mined.

Is it therefore worthwhile investing in cryptocurrencies in 2021?

Investing in cryptocurrencies today certainly offers an excellent opportunity to benefit from the high growth potential of these assets in the medium to long term. Cryptocurrencies are increasingly seen as alternatives to traditional currencies, and will benefit from the growing adoption of blockchains in the real economy. Among the main advantages of cryptocurrencies there is that of not depending on a central authority, such as a government or a bank. Some cryptocurrencies, such as Bitcoin, have a fixed supply amount and this makes them particularly attractive as a safe haven asset against inflation and financial risks. The best way to invest in cryptocurrencies is through an exchange or through a trading platform offered by a regulated and licensed broker.

Among the most effective strategies for investing in cryptocurrencies is diversification, i.e., investing in multiple cryptocurrencies, and the gradual increase of your investment to take advantage of the phases of volatility.

Investing In Cryptocurrencies - Frequently Asked Questions

What are cryptocurrencies? A cryptocurrency is a digital currency that uses blockchain technology to validate online transactions through decentralized systems. Thanks to the blockchain, all cryptocurrency transactions are transparent, safe, easy to track and irreversible.

How to invest in cryptocurrencies? There are two main ways to invest in cryptocurrencies. When you buy cryptocurrency at one of the best exchanges, you effectively own the cryptocurrency and can store it in a wallet. With a trading platform you can instead trade CFDs and speculate on price movements.

What are the secrets to investing in crypto? The first thing to do is to understand the concept of cryptocurrency well and analyze the market. Once you decide to invest in cryptocurrencies, it is important to diversify, buying multiple assets and take advantage of periods of volatility by increasing the investment at more advantageous prices.

Is it worth investing in cryptocurrencies? Looking at how Bitcoin has risen, and how many new cryptocurrencies are springing up every month, definitely yes. This kind of asset represents the evolution of classic coins and the future will be dominated by them.

How much does it cost to invest in cryptocurrencies? The costs depend on the platform used. Generally, there are brokers, such as eToro, or exchanges that ask for less than 1% as a commission cost.

www.ingramcontent.com/pod-product-compliance
Lightning Source LLC
Chambersburg PA
CBHW061049050326
40690CB00012B/2565